The Kids' Music Collection

Songs compiled in this collection were very carefully selected for the "kid" in all of us. From our favorite nursery rhymes to the positive, uplifting "I Believe I Can Fly," all of these songs will bring hours of playing pleasure for Moms, Dads, big brothers and sisters, baby-sitters, day care teachers and even Grandmas and Grandpas. This book can be passed on from generation to generation because this music will always have a place in our childhood memories.

...Editor

WARNER BROS. PUBLICATIONS - THE GLOBAL LEADER IN PRINT
USA: 15800 NW 48th Avenue, Miami, FL 33014

WARNER/CHAPPELL MUSIC

CANADA: 85 SCARSDALE ROAD, SUITE 101
DON MILLS, ONTARIO, M3B 2R2
SCANDINAVIA: P.O. BOX 533, VENDEVAGEN 85 B
S-182 15, DANDERYD, SWEDEN
AUSTRALIA: P.O. BOX 353
3 TALAVERA ROAD, NORTH RYDE N.S.W. 2113

Carisch
NUOVA CARISCH

ITALY: VIA CAMPANIA, 12
20098 S. GIULIANO MILANESE (MI)
ZONA INDUSTRIALE SESTO ULTERIANO
SPAIN: MAGALLANES, 25
28015 MADRID
FRANCE: 25 RUE DE HAUTEVILLE, 75010 PARIS

IMP
INTERNATIONAL MUSIC PUBLICATIONS LIMITED

ENGLAND: SOUTHEND ROAD,
WOODFORD GREEN, ESSEX IG8 8HN
GERMANY: MARSTALLSTR. 8, D-80539 MUNCHEN
DENMARK: DANMUSIK, VOGNMAGERGADE 7
DK 1120 KOBENHAVNK

Editor/Project Manager: Carol Cuellar
Book Design: Joseph Klucar / Jorge Paredes

CARTOON FAVORITES

PARTY & PLAY

PATRIOTIC FAVORITES

POPULAR FAVORITES

MOVIE & TV HITS

Cartoon Favorites

From the Motion Picture "BATMAN" ™

THE BATMAN THEME

Music Composed by
DANNY ELFMAN
Arranged by DAN COATES

Moderately Slow

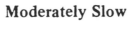

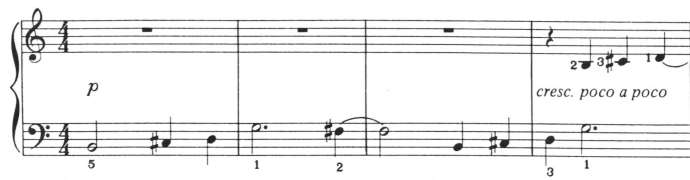

The Batman Theme - 5 - 1

8

The Batman Theme - 5 - 3

(MEET) THE FLINTSTONES
(from THE FLINTSTONES)

Words and Music by
WILLIAM HANNA, JOSEPH BARBERA
and HOYT CURTIN
Arranged by DAN COATES

I TAUT I TAW A PUDDY-TAT
(I Thought I Saw a Pussy-Cat)

Words and Music by
ALAN LIVINGSTON, BILLY MAY and WARREN FOSTER
Arranged by DAN COATES

I Taut I Taw a Puddy-Tat - 2 - 1

2. There is a great big bad old cat,
   Sylvester is his name,
   He only has one aim in life
   And that is very plain.
   He dreams of catching Tweety Pie
   And eating him one day,
   But just as he gets close enough,
   Tweety gets away. *(Chorus:)*

3. Tweety sometimes takes a walk
   And goes outside his cage,
   But he gets back before the cat
   And throws him in a rage.
   Sylvester'd love to eat that bird
   If he could just get near.
   But everytime that he comes by,
   This is all he'll hear: *(Chorus:)*

4. And when he sings that little song,
   His mistress knows he's home.
   She grabs her broom and brings it down
   Upon Sylvester's dome.
   So there's no need of worrying,
   He lives just like a king,
   And puddy tat's can't hurt that bird
   As long as he can sing: *(Chorus:)*

THE JETSONS MAIN THEME
from "THE JETSONS"

Words and Music by WILLIAM HANNA,
JOSEPH BARBERA and HOYT S. CURTIN
Arranged by DAN COATES

The Jetsons Main Theme - 2 - 1

From the TV Show "PEANUTS SPECIAL"

LINUS AND LUCY

By VINCE GUARALDI
Arranged by DAN COATES

Linus and Lucy - 2 - 1

Linus and Lucy - 2 - 2

MERRILY WE ROLL ALONG

Words and Music by
EDDIE CANTOR, MURRAY MENCHER
and CHARLIE TOBIAS
Arranged by DAN COATES

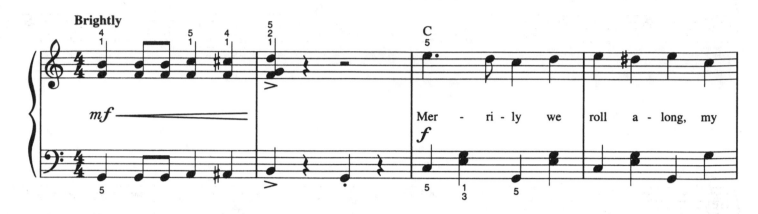

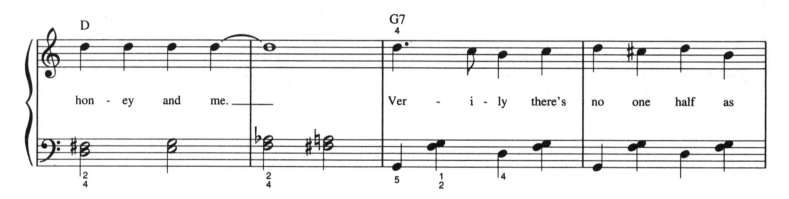

Merrily We Roll Along - 2 - 1

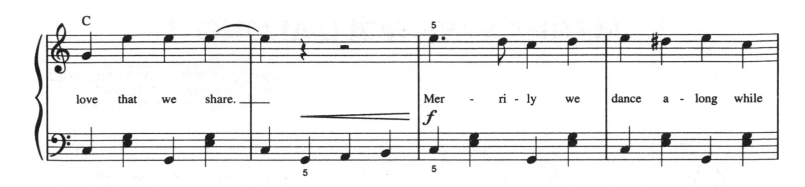

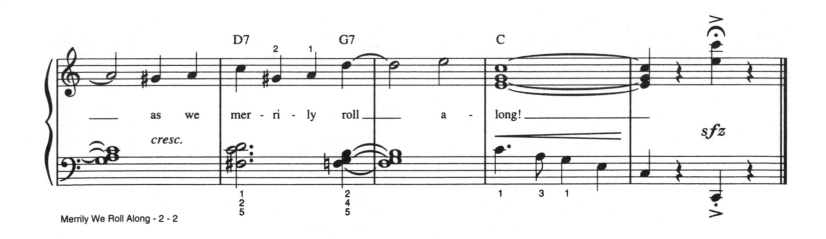

THE MERRY-GO-ROUND BROKE DOWN

Words and Music by
CLIFF FRIEND and DAVE FRANKLIN
Arranged by DAN COATES

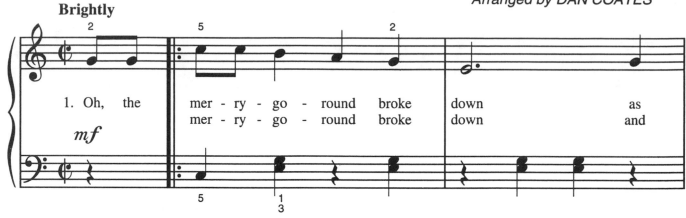

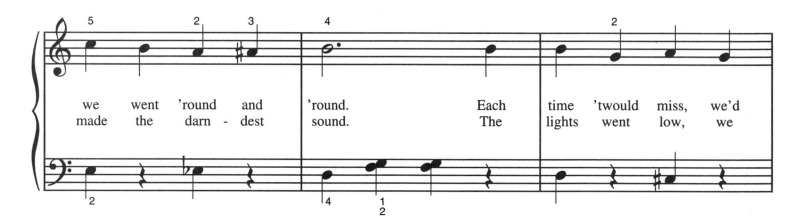

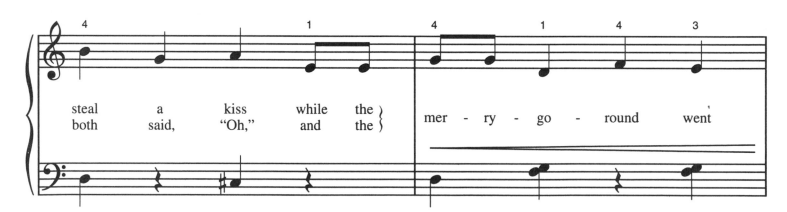

The Merry-Go-Round Broke Down - 3 - 1

um - pah - pah. 2. The   um - pah - pah.   Oh,   what

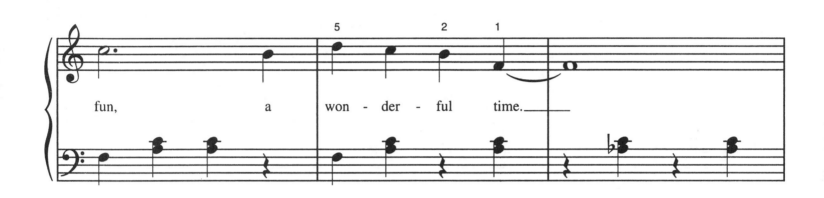

fun,   a   won - der - ful   time.

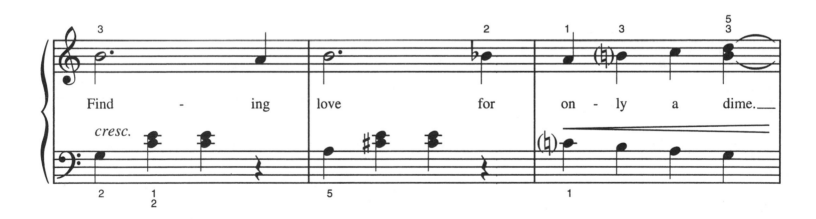

Find - ing   love   for   on - ly   a   dime.

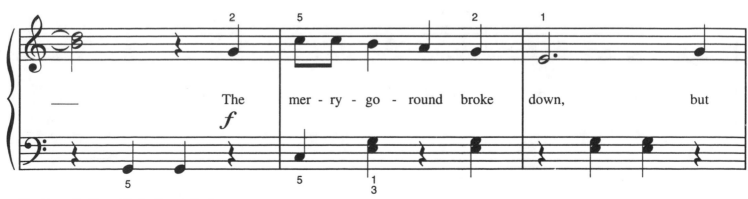

The   mer - ry - go - round   broke   down,   but

The Merry-Go-Round Broke Down - 3 - 2

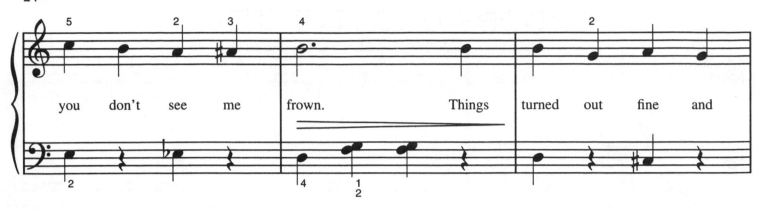

you don't see me   frown.   Things   turned   out   fine   and

now   she's   mine,   'cause the   mer - ry - go - round   went

um - pah - pah,   um - pah - pah,   um - pah,   um - pah,

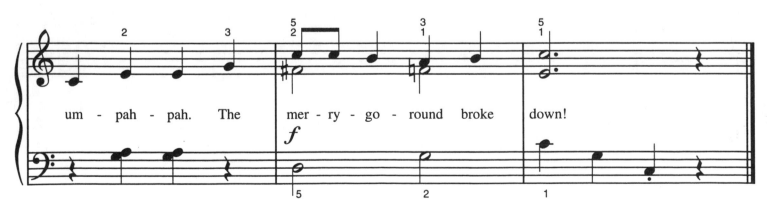

um - pah - pah. The   mer - ry - go - round   broke   down!

SCOOBY DOO MAIN TITLE
from the Cartoon Television Series

Words and Music by
WILLIAM HANNA, JOSEPH BARBERA
and HOYT CURTAIN
Arranged by DAN COATES

THEME FROM INSPECTOR GADGET
(Animated Cartoon Series)

Words and Music by
HAIM SABAN and SHUKI LEVY
Arranged by DAN COATES

Theme from Inspector Gadget - 4 - 1

28

Theme from Inspector Gadget - 4 - 3

Theme from Inspector Gadget - 4 - 4

THEME FROM "THE SIMPSONS"

Music by
DANNY ELFMAN
Arranged by DAN COATES

Moderately Fast (♩ = 168)

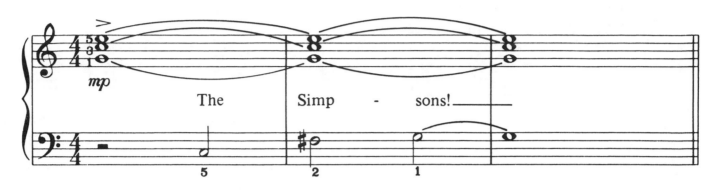

The Simp - sons!

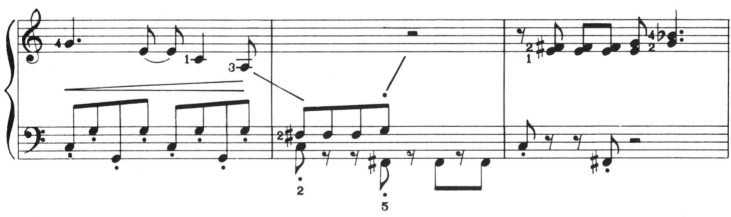

Theme from "The Simpsons" - 4 - 1

Theme from "The Simpsons" - 4 - 2

Theme from "The Simpsons" - 4 - 3

Theme from "The Simpsons" - 4 - 4

Theme from "THE BUGS BUNNY SHOW"

THIS IS IT!

Words and Music by
MACK DAVID and JERRY LIVINGSTON
Arranged by DAN COATES

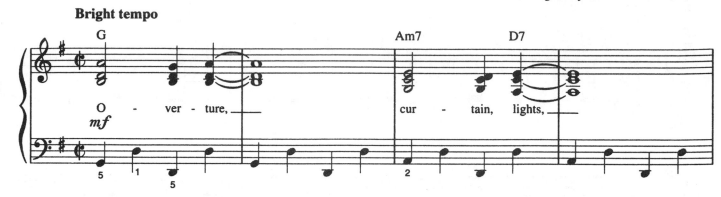

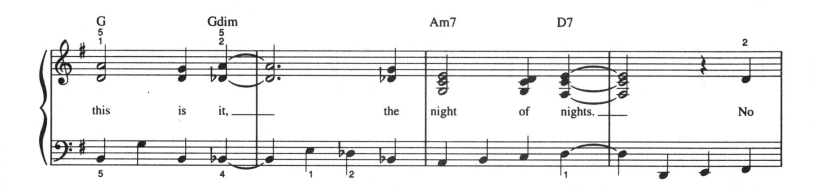

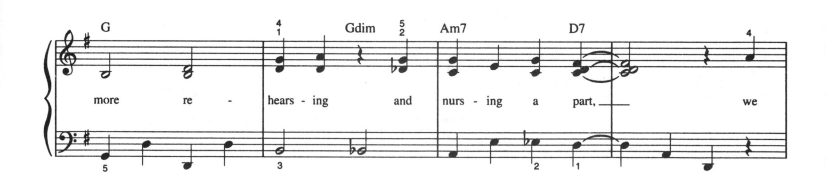

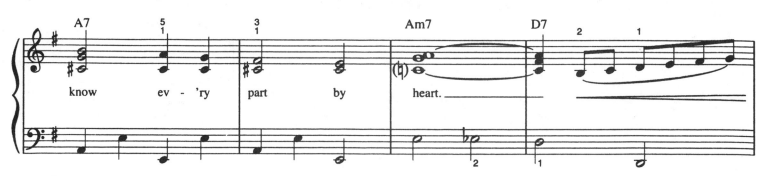

This Is It! - 2 - 1

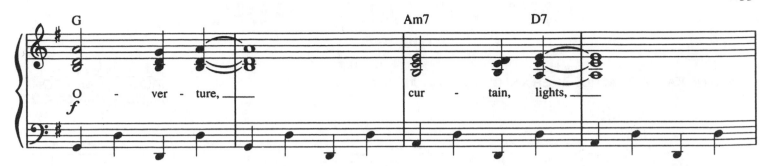

This Is It! - 2 - 2

TINY TOON ADVENTURES
Theme Song

Lyrics by
WAYNE KAATZ, TOM RUEGGER and BRUCE BROUGHTON

Music by
BRUCE BROUGHTON
Arranged by DAN COATES

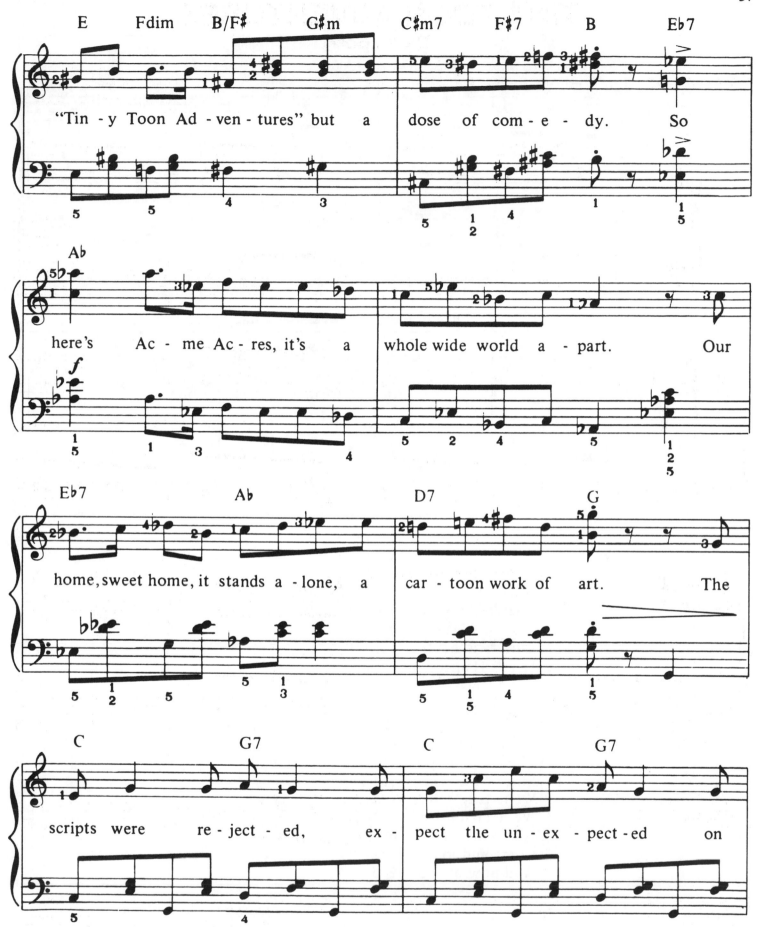

Extra Lyrics

2. They're furry, they're funny,
   They're Babs and Buster Bunny,
   Montana Max has money,
   Elmyra is a pain.
   Here's Hamton and Plucky,
   Dizzy Devil's yucky.
   Furball's unlucky
   And Go-Go is insane.
   At Acme Looniversity we earn our toon degree.
   The teaching staff's been getting laughs
   Since Nineteen Thirty-Three.
   We're tiny, we're tooney,
   We're all a little looney.
   It's "Tiny Toon Adventures"
   Come and join the fun.
   And now our song is done!

Party & Play Songs

"C" IS FOR COOKIE

Words and Music by
JOE RAPOSO
Arranged by DAN COATES

THE CHICKEN DANCE
(DANCE LITTLE BIRD)

English Lyric
by PAUL PARNES

By TERRY RENDALL
and WERNER THOMAS
Arranged by DAN COATES

The Chicken Dance - 3 - 1

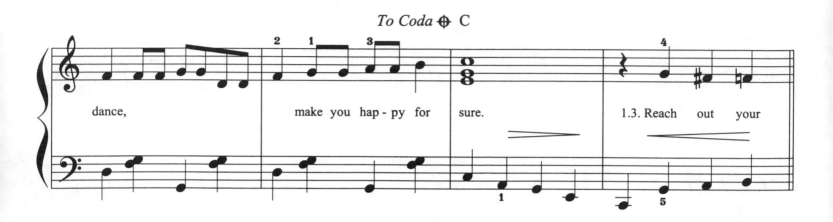

Chorus:

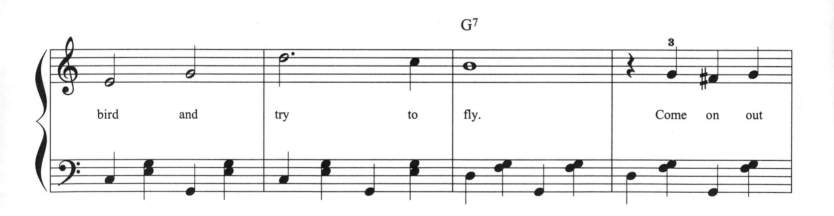

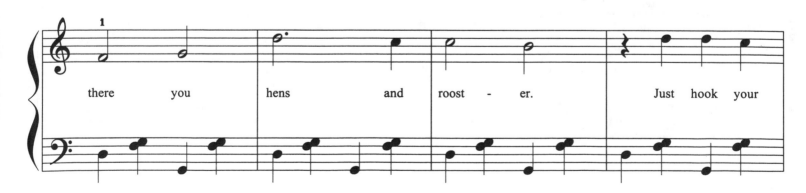

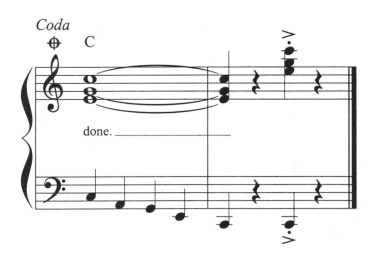

Verse 2:
Hey, you're in the swing.
You're cluckin' like a bird. (Pluck, pluck, pluck, pluck.)
You're flappin' your wings.
Don't you feel absurd? (No, no, no, no.)
It's a chicken dance,
Like a rooster and a hen. (Ya, ya, ya, ya.)
Flappy chicken dance,
Let's do it again. *(To Chorus 2:)*

Chorus 2:
Relax and let the music move you.
Let all your inhibitions go.
Just watch your partner whirl around you.
We're having fun now, I told you so.

Verse 3:
Now you're flapping like a bird
And you're wigglin' too. (I like that move.)
You're without a care.
It's a dance for you. (Just made for you.)
Keep doin' what you do.
Don't you cop out now. (Don't cop out now.)
Gets better as you dance,
Catch your breath somehow. *(To Chorus 3:)*

Verse 4:
Now we're almost through,
Really flyin' high. (Bye, bye, bye, bye.)
All you chickens and birds,
Time to say goodbye. (To say goodbye.)
Goin' back to the nest,
But the flyin' was fun. (Oh, it was fun.)
Chicken dance was the best,
But the dance is done!

MACARENA

Words and Music by
ANTONIO ROMERO and RAFAEL RUIZ
Arranged by DAN COATES

Macarena - 4 - 1

MAIRZY DOATS

Words and Music by
JERRY LIVINGSTON, MILTON DRAKE
and AL HOFFMAN
Arranged by DAN COATES

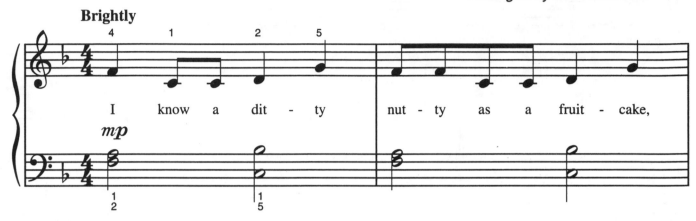

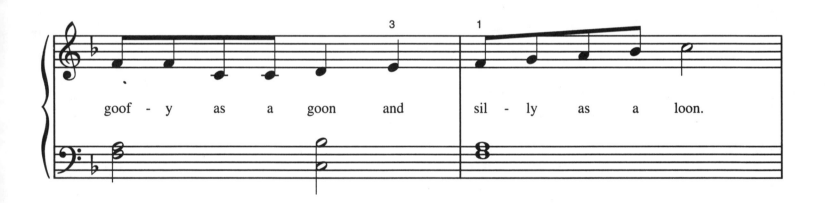

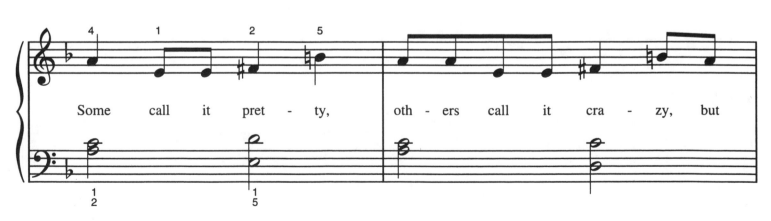

Mairzy Doats - 4 - 1

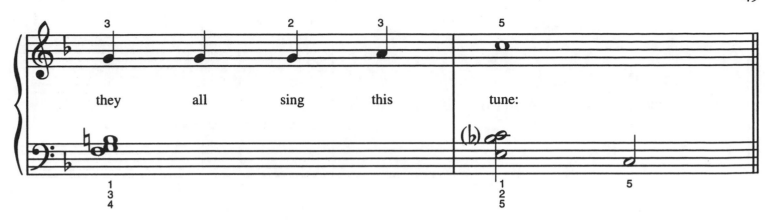

they all sing this tune:

Chorus:

Mair - zy doats and do - zy doats and lid - dle lam - zy div - ey, a

mf

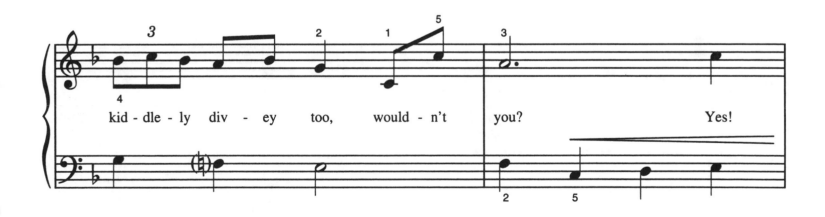

kid - dle - ly div - ey too, would - n't you? Yes!

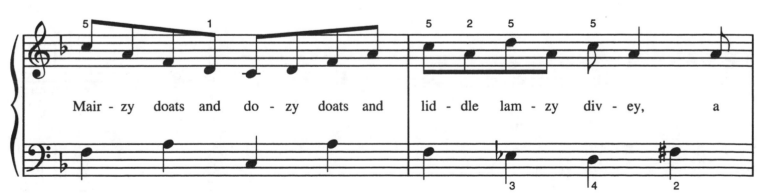

Mair - zy doats and do - zy doats and lid - dle lam - zy div - ey, a

*In this section, ♫ may be played as ♪. ♪

Mairzy Doats - 4 - 2

kid - dle - ly div - ey too, would - n't you? If the

words sound queer and fun - ny to your ear, a

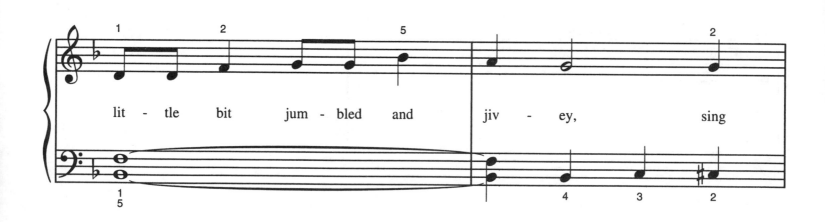

lit - tle bit jum - bled and jiv - ey, sing

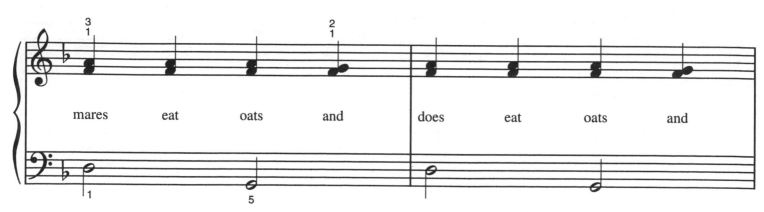

mares eat oats and does eat oats and

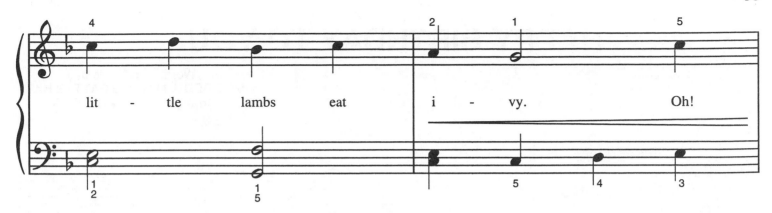

lit - tle   lambs   eat   i - vy.   Oh!

Mair - zy doats and do - zy doats and lid - dle lam - zy div - ey,   a

f

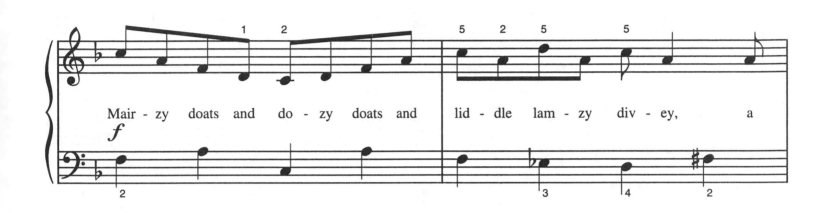

kid - dle - ly div - ey too, would - n't you?_____   A

kid - dle - ly div - ey too, would - n't you?

Mairzy Doats - 4 - 4

HAPPY BIRTHDAY TO YOU!

Words and Music by
MILDRED J. HILL and PATTYS HILL
Arranged by DAN COATES

[*Insert name here]

Patriotic Favorites

AMERICA THE BEAUTIFUL

Words by
KATHERINE LEE BATES

Music by
SAMUEL A. WARD
Arranged by DAN COATES

Slowly, with expression

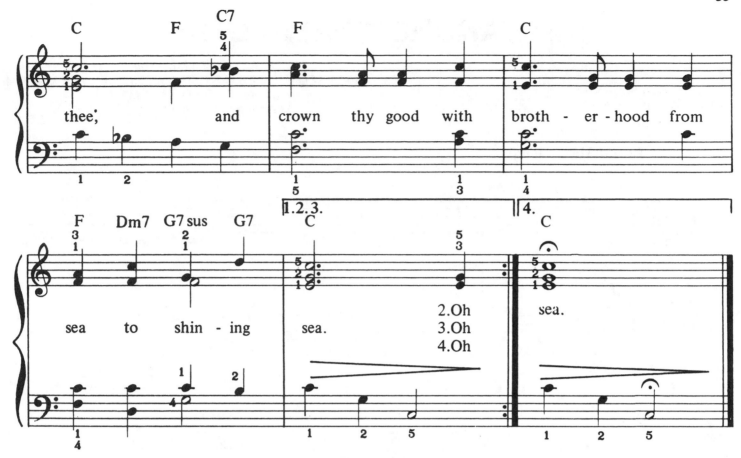

Extra Lyrics:

Verse 2. Oh beautiful for pilgrim feet
Whose stern impassioned stress
A thoroughfare for freedom beat
Across the wilderness.

Chorus: America! America! God mend thine ev'ry flaw.
Confirm thy soul in self-control,
Thy liberty in law.

Verse 3. Oh beautiful for heroes proved
In liberating strife.
Who more than self their country loved,
And mercy more than life.

Chorus: America! America! May God tho gold refine
Till all success be nobleness
And ev'ry gain, divine.

Verse 4. Oh beautiful for patriot dream
That sees beyond the years.
Thine alabaster cities gleam.
Undimm'd by human tears.

Chorus: America! America! God shed His grace on thee,
And crown thy good with brotherhood
From sea to shining sea.

ANCHORS AWEIGH

Words and Music by
Captain ALFRED H. MILES U.S.N.(Ret.), CHARLES A. ZIMMERMAN
and GEORGE D. LOTTMAN
Arranged by DAN COATES

Bright March tempo

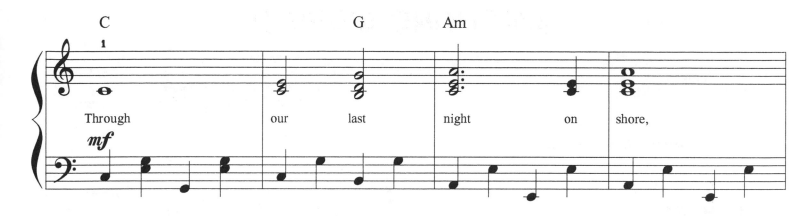

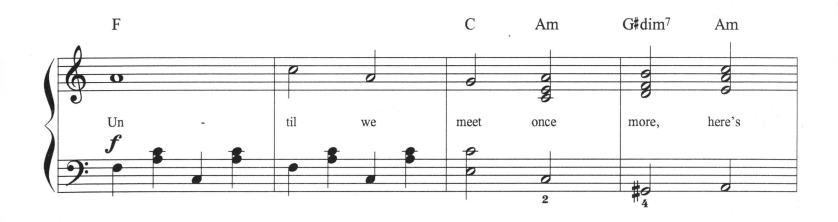

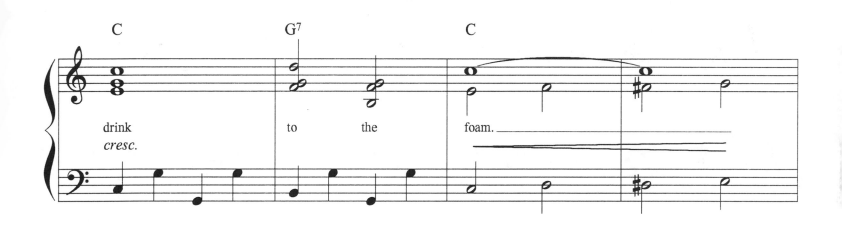

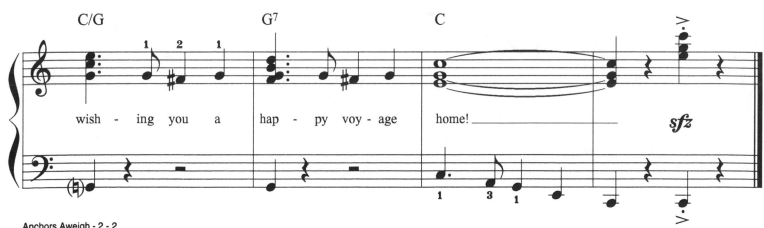

THE STAR-SPANGLED BANNER

Words by
FRANCIS SCOTT KEY

Music by
JOHN STAFFORD SMITH
Arranged by DAN COATES

The Star-Spangled Banner - 2 - 2

AMERICA
(My Country 'Tis of Thee)

Words by
REV. SAMUEL F. SMITH

TRADITIONAL MELODY
Arranged by DAN COATES

Popular Favorites

FUZZY WUZZY

Words and Music by
JERRY LIVINGSTON, AL HOFFMAN
and MILTON DRAKE
Arranged by DAN COATES

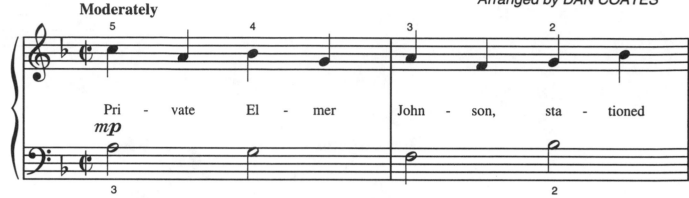

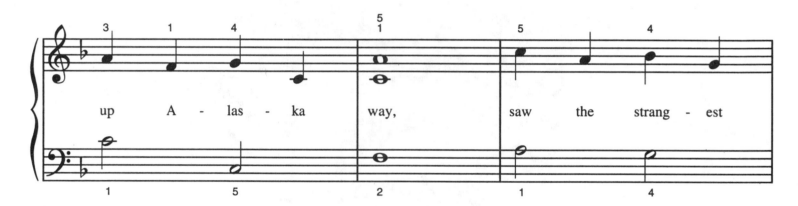

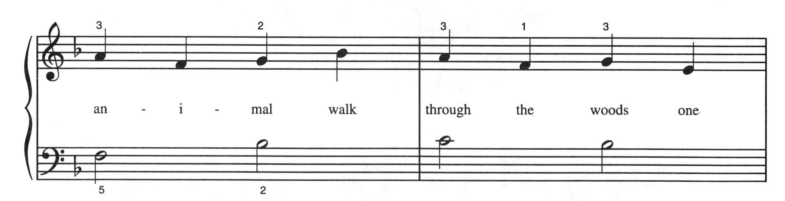

Fuzzy Wuzzy - 4 - 1

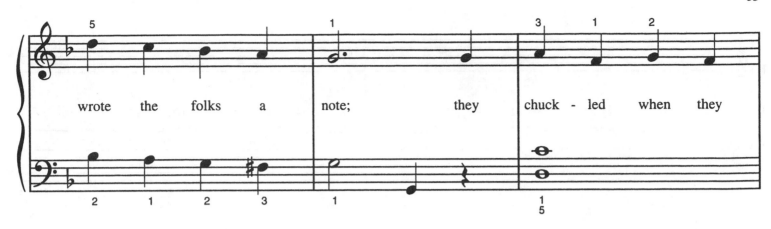

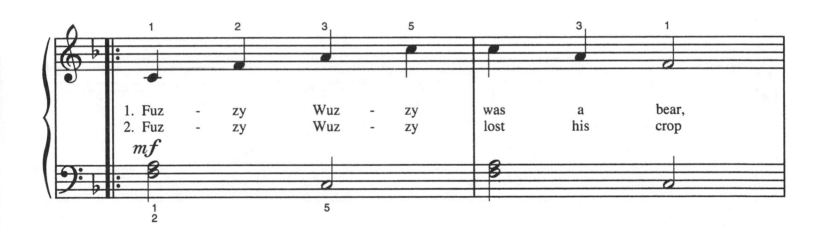

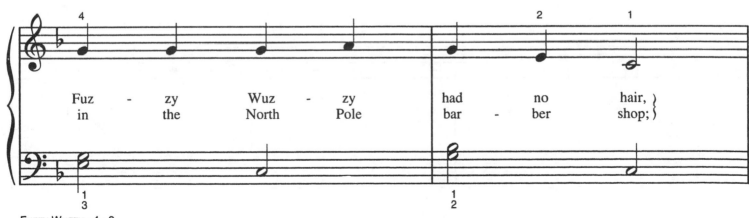

Fuzzy Wuzzy - 4 - 2

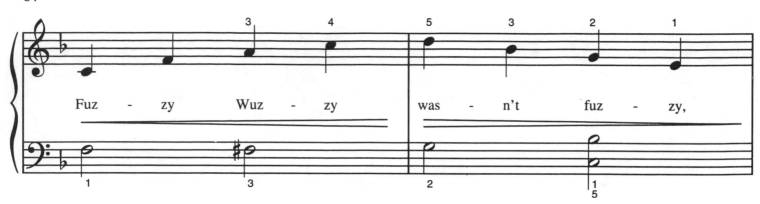

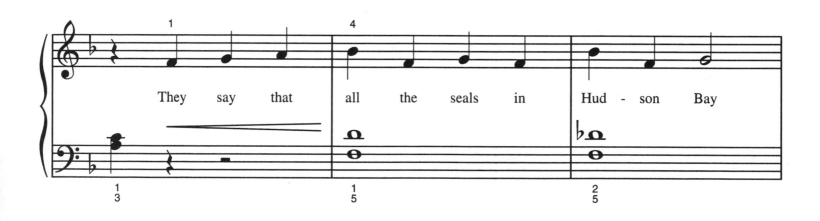

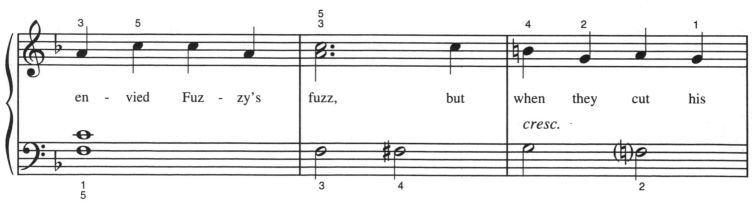

Fuzzy Wuzzy - 4 - 3

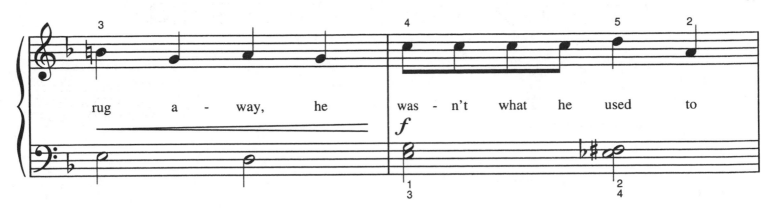

rug a - way, he was - n't what he used to

wuz! Cuz Fuz - zy Wuz - zy was a bear,

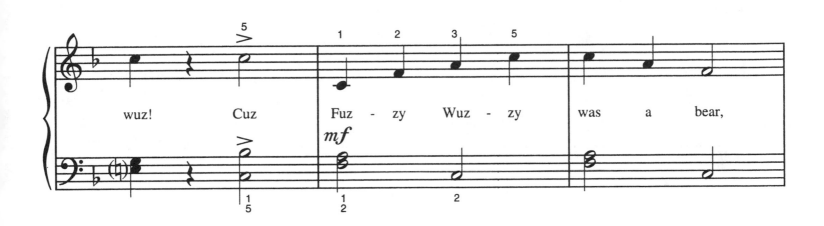

Fuz - zy Wuz - zy had no hair, Fuz - zy Wuz - zy

was - n't fuz - zy, wuz he?

Fuzzy Wuzzy - 4 - 4

I'D LIKE TO TEACH THE WORLD TO SING
(In Perfect Harmony)

Words and Music by
B. BACKER, B. DAVIS,
R. COOK and R. GREENAWAY
Arranged by DAN COATES

Moderate swing tempo

I'd Like to Teach the World to Sing - 2 - 1

LITTLE SIR ECHO

Original Version by LAURA R. SMITH and J.S. FEARIS
Words and Revised Arrangement by
ADELE GIRARD and JOE MARSALA
Arranged by DAN COATES

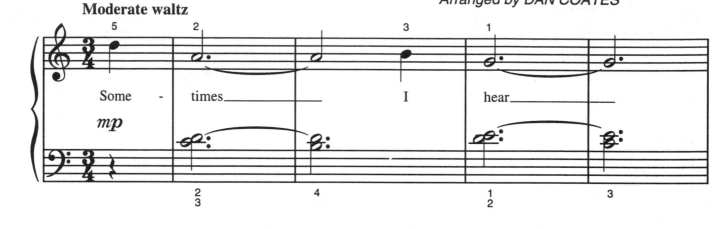

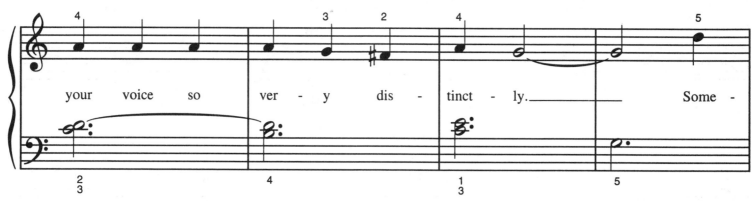

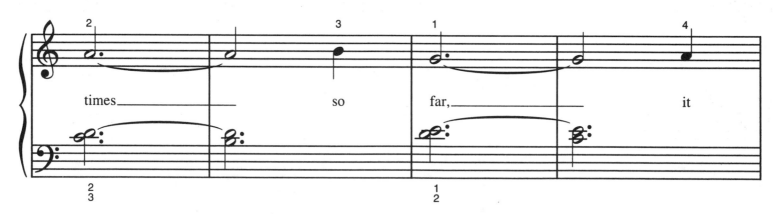

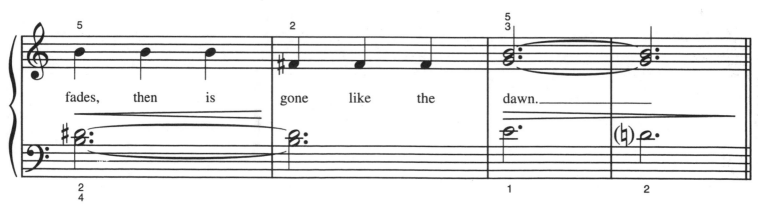

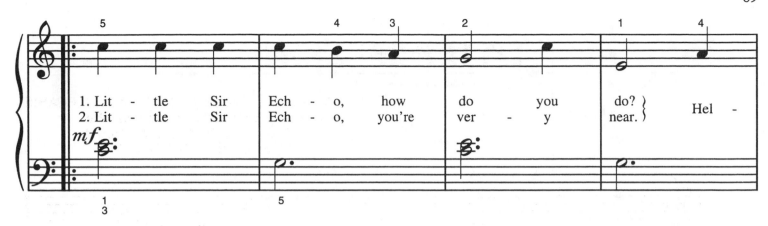

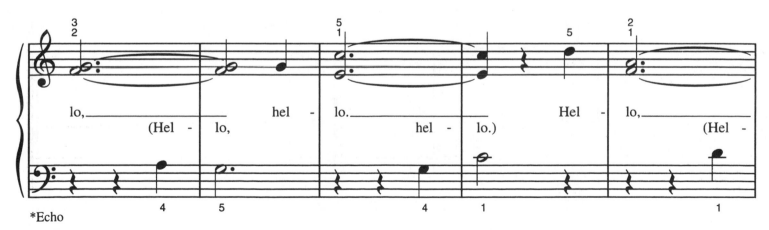

*Echo

Little Sir Echo - 3 - 2

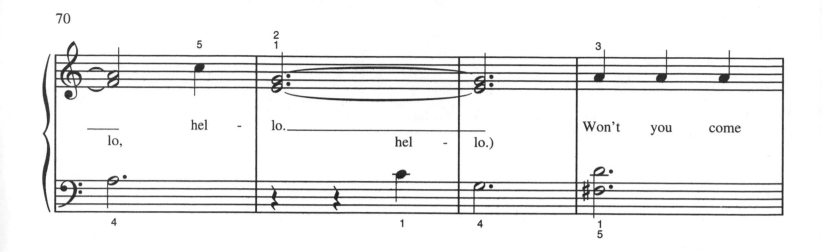

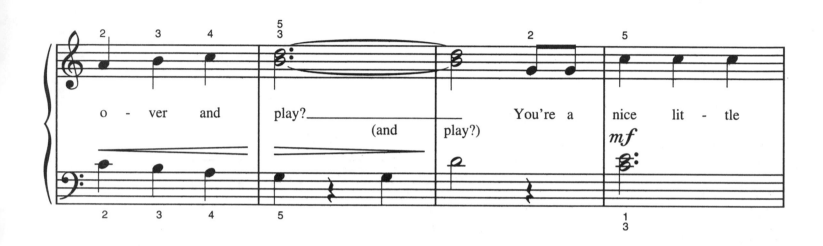

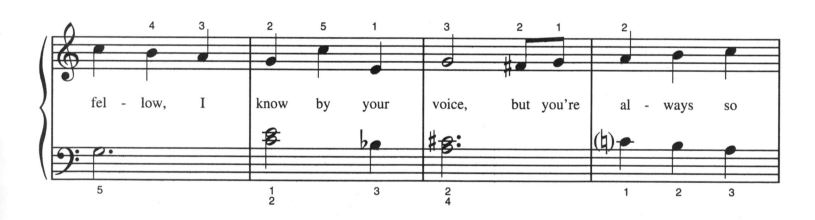

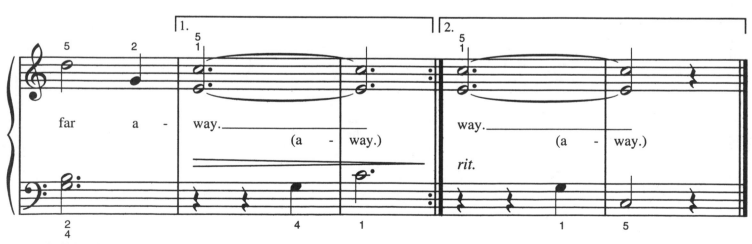

Little Sir Echo - 3 - 3

MUSIC BOX DANCER

Music by
FRANK MILLS
Arranged by DAN COATES

Music Box Dancer - 3 - 1

72

Music Box Dancer - 3 - 3

PUFF
(THE MAGIC DRAGON)

Words and Music by
PETER YARROW and LEONARD LIPTON
Arranged by DAN COATES

Puff, the mag - ic drag - on, lived by the
2.3.4. *See additional lyrics*

sea and frol - icked in the au - tumn mist in a

land called Hon - ah - lee. Lit - tle Jack - ie Pa - per

loved that ras - cal Puff, and brought him strings and

Puff (the Magic Dragon) - 3 - 1

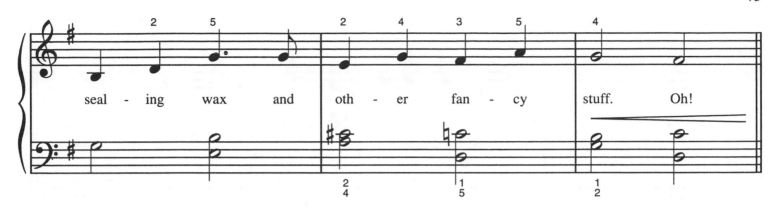

seal - ing wax and oth - er fan - cy stuff. Oh!

Chorus:

Puff, the mag - ic drag - on, lived by the sea and

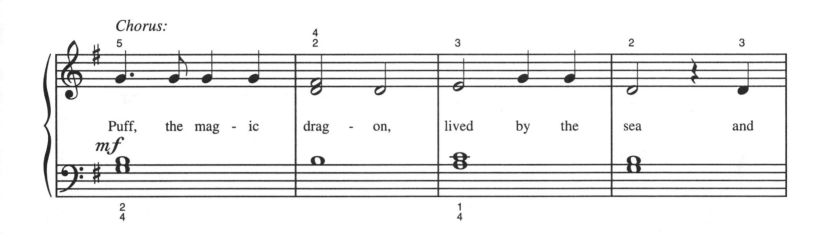

frol - icked in the au - tumn mist in a land called Hon - ah - lee.

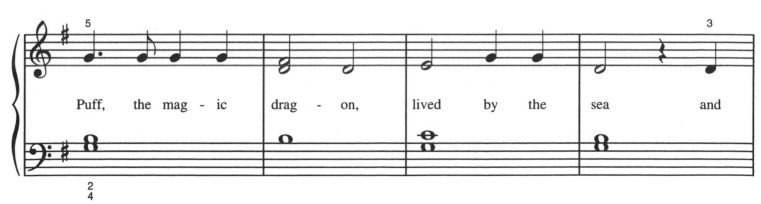

Puff, the mag - ic drag - on, lived by the sea and

Puff (the Magic Dragon) - 3 - 2

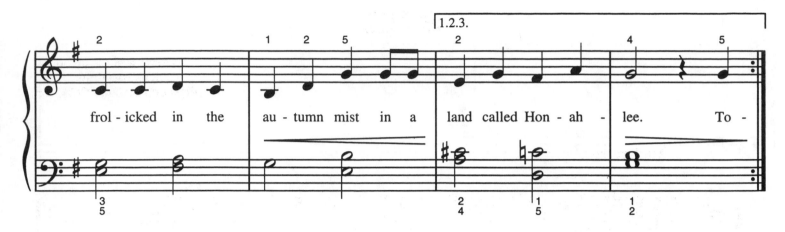

frol - icked in the au - tumn mist in a land called Hon - ah - lee. To -

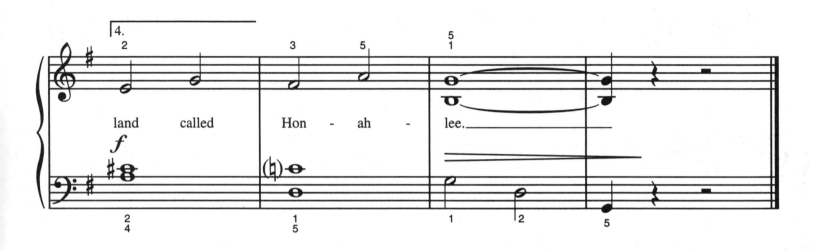

land called Hon - ah - lee.

Verse 2:
Together they would travel on a boat with billowed sail,
Jackie left a lookout perched on Puff's gigantic tail.
Noble kings and princes would bow when'er they came.
Pirate ships would low'r their flag when Puff roared out his name. Oh!
(To Chorus:)

Verse 3:
A dragon lives forever, but not so little boys;
Painted wings and giant rings make way for other toys.
One grey night it happened, Jackie Paper came no more,
And Puff, that mighty dragon, he ceased his fearless roar. Oh!
(To Chorus:)

Verse 4:
His head was bent in sorrow, green scales fell like rain,
Puff not longer went to play along the cherry lane.
Without his life-long friend, Puff could not be brave,
So Puff, that mighty dragon, sadly slipped into his cave. Oh!
(To Chorus:)

SING

Words and Music by
JOE RAPOSO
Arranged by DAN COATES

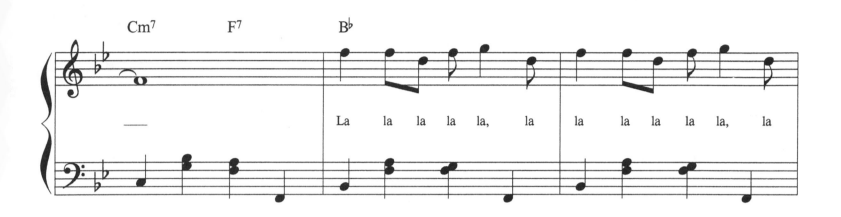

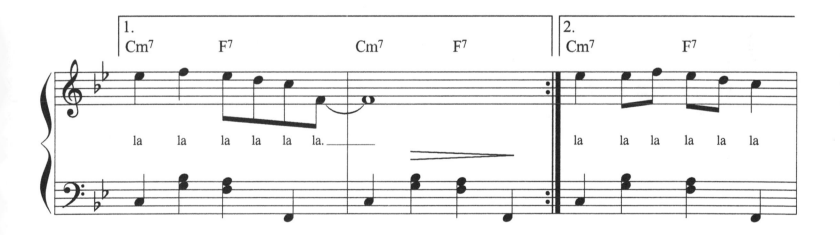

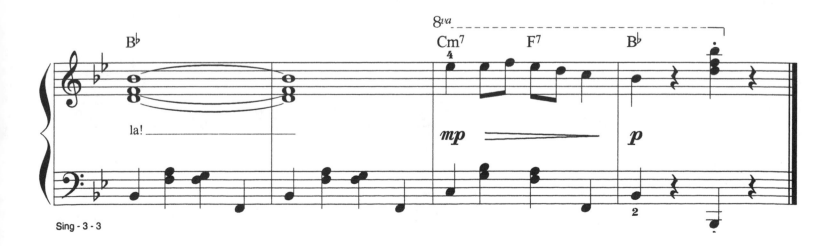

Sing - 3 - 3

THE SONG THAT DOESN'T END

Music and Lyrics by
NORMAN MARTIN
Arranged by DAN COATES

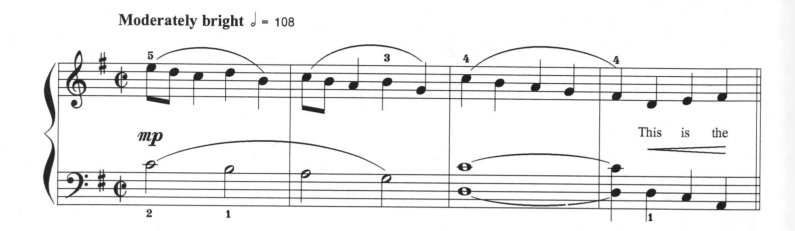

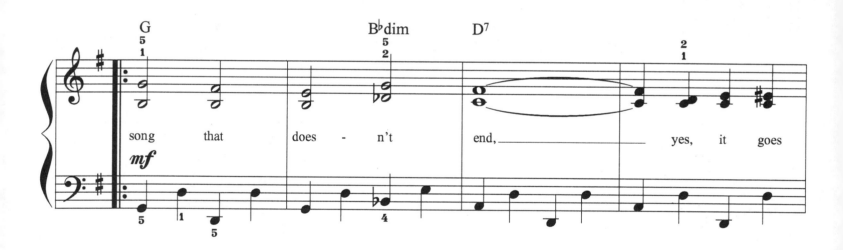

The Song That Doesn't End - 3 - 1

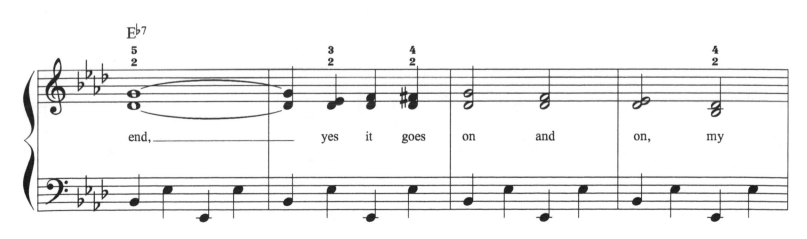

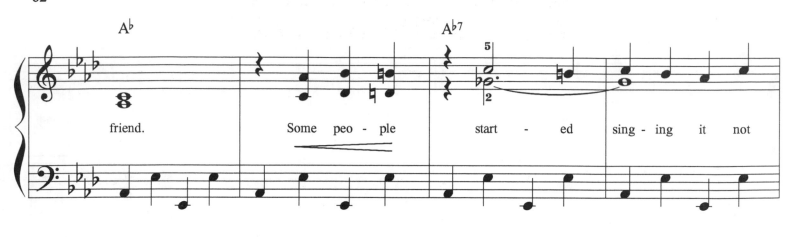

friend. Some peo-ple start-ed sing-ing it not

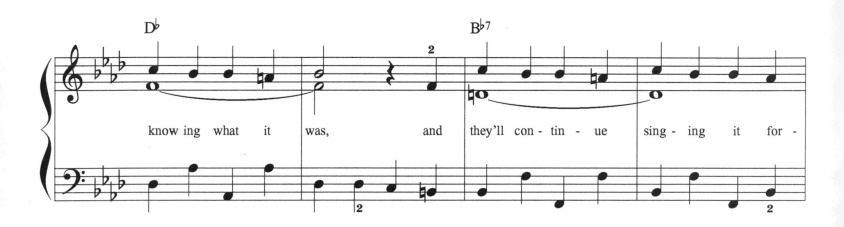

know ing what it was, and they'll con-tin-ue sing-ing it for-

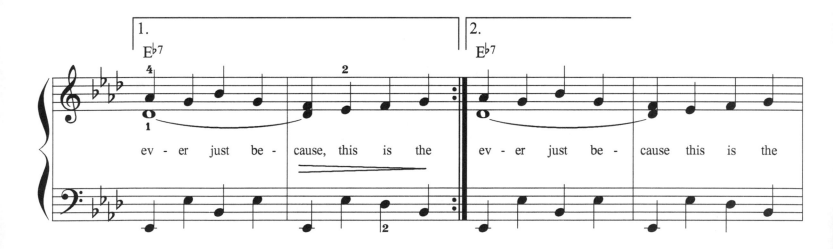

1.
ev-er just be-cause, this is the

2.
ev-er just be-cause this is the

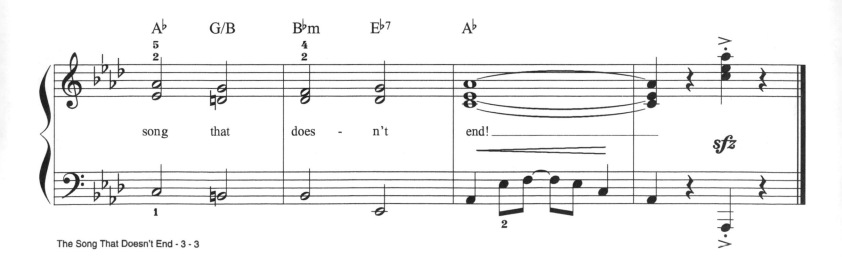

song that does - n't end! _____

From the Motion Picture "DOCTOR DOLITTLE"

TALK TO THE ANIMALS

Words and Music by
LESLIE BRICUSSE
Arranged by DAN COATES

Talk to the Animals - 3 - 1

TAKE ME OUT TO THE BALL GAME

Words by
JACK NORWORTH

Music by
ALBERT VON TILZER
Arranged by DAN COATES

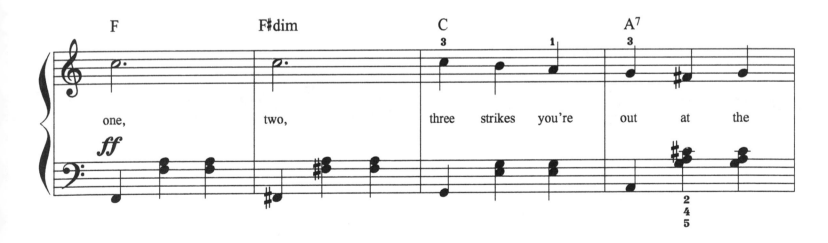

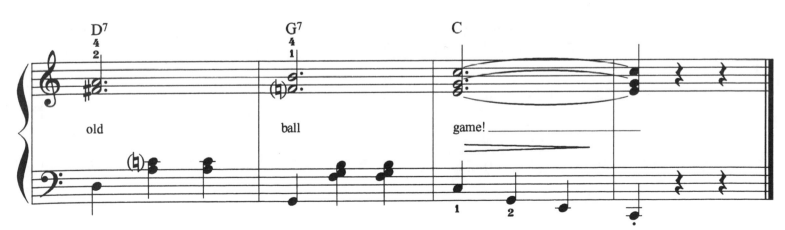

Take Me Out to the Ball Game - 2 - 2

THE TEDDY BEARS' PICNIC

Words by
JIMMY KENNEDY

Music by
JOHN W. BRATTON
Arranged by DAN COATES

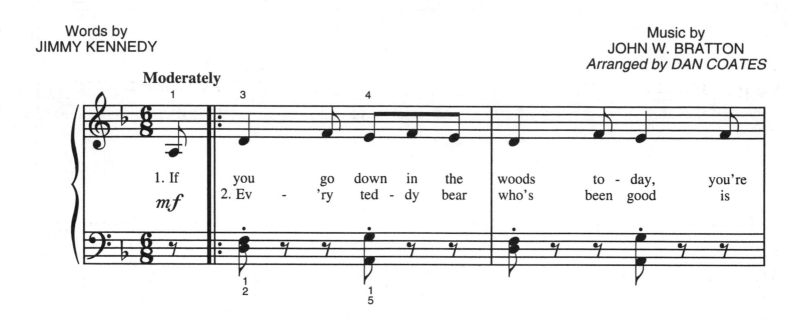

1. If you go down in the woods to-day, you're
2. Ev-'ry ted-dy bear who's been good is

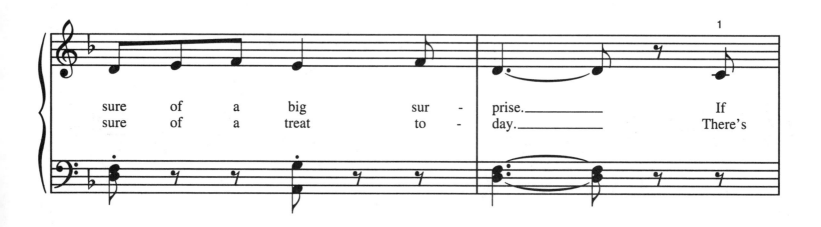

sure of a big sur-prise. If
sure of a treat to-day. There's

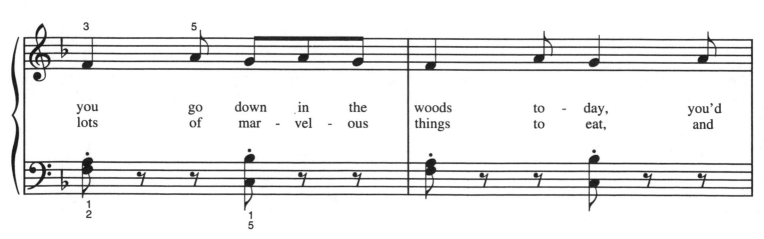

you go down in the woods to-day, you'd
lots of mar-vel-ous things to eat, and

The Teddy Bears' Picnic - 5 - 1

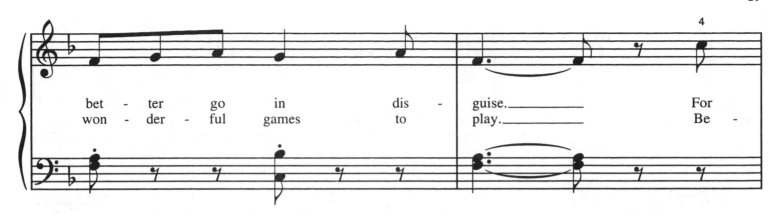

bet - ter go in dis - guise._____ For
won - der - ful games to play._____ Be -

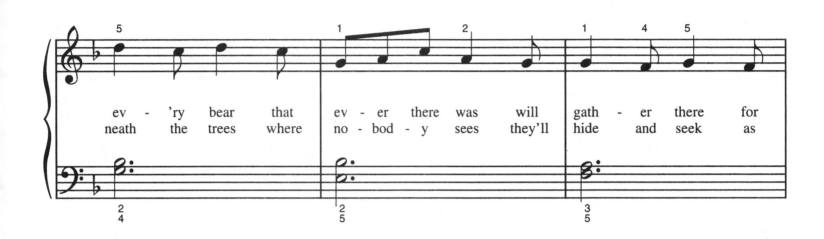

ev - 'ry bear that ev - er there was will gath - er there for
neath the trees where no - bod - y sees they'll hide and seek as

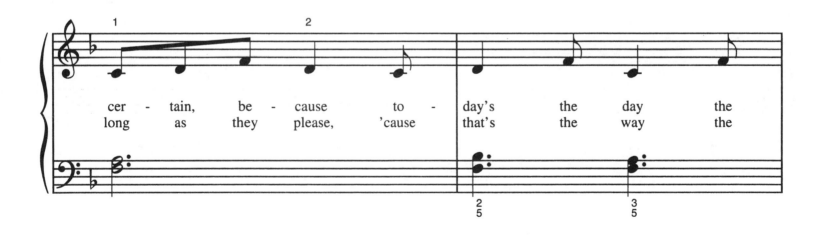

cer - tain, be - cause to - day's the day the
long as they please, 'cause that's the way the

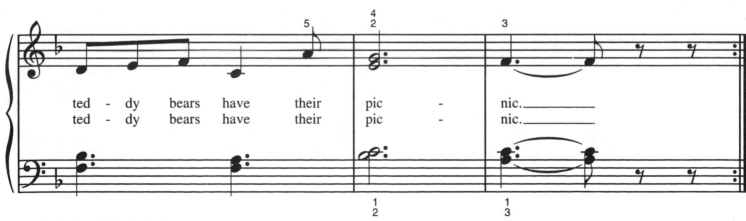

ted - dy bears have their pic - nic._____
ted - dy bears have their pic - nic._____

The Teddy Bears' Picnic - 5 - 2

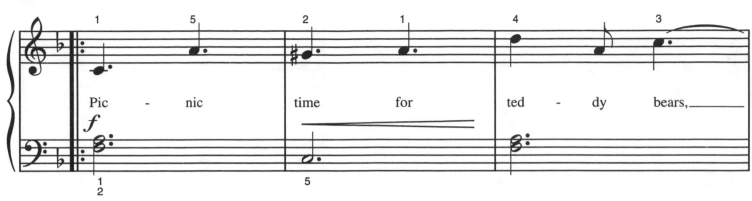

Pic - nic time for ted - dy bears,_____

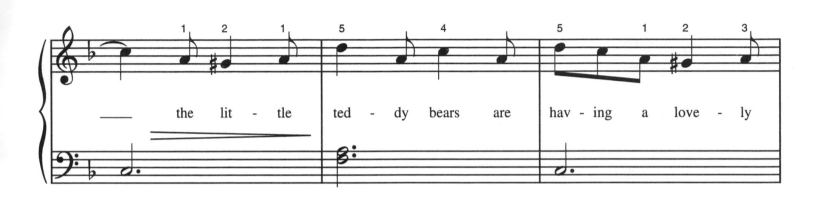

_____ the lit - tle ted - dy bears are hav - ing a love - ly

time to - day. Watch them,

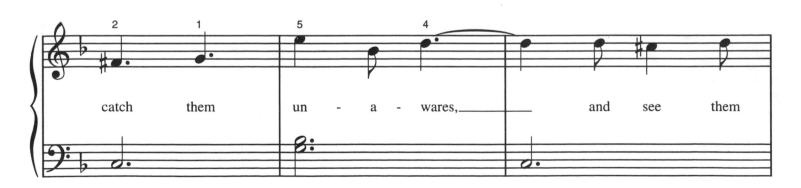

catch them un - a - wares,_____ and see them

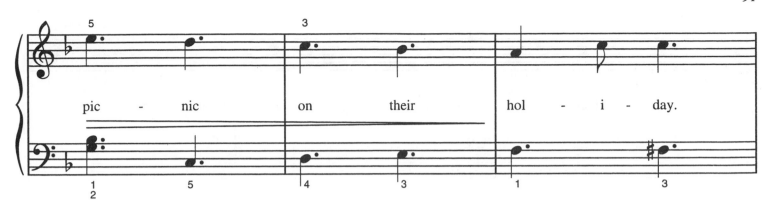

pic - nic   on their   hol - i - day.

See   them   gai - ly

gad a - bout,____   they love to   play and shout; they

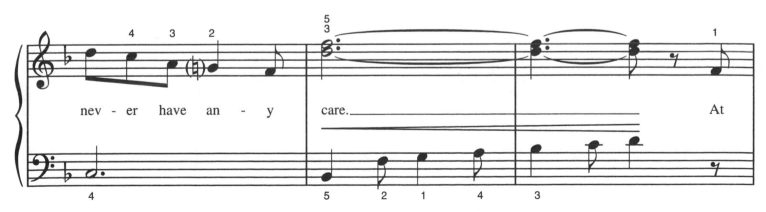

nev - er have an - y   care.____   At

The Teddy Bears' Picnic - 5 - 4

six o'-clock their mum-mies and dad-dies will take them home to

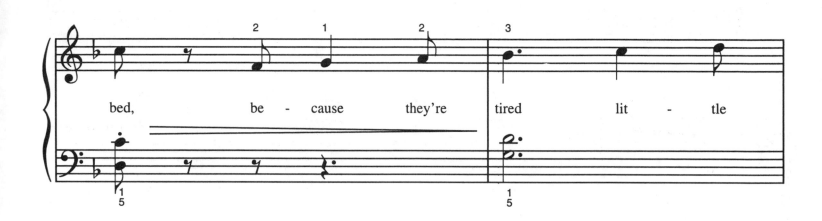

bed, be - cause they're tired lit - tle

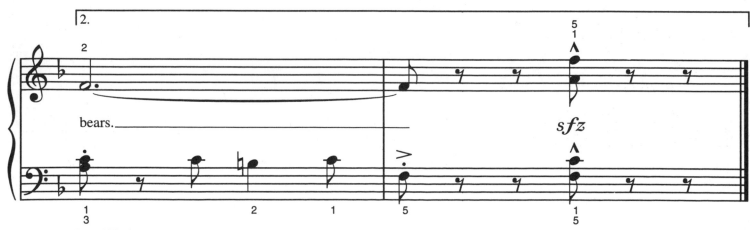

1.

ted - dy bears.

2.

bears.

sfz

From the Motion Picture "ANNIE"

TOMORROW

Lyrics by
MARTIN CHARNIN

Music by
CHARLES STROUSE
Arranged by DAN COATES

Movie & TV Hits

Theme from "GILLIGAN'S ISLAND" TV Series

THE BALLAD OF GILLIGAN'S ISLE

Words and Music by
SHERWOOD SCHWARTZ and GEORGE WYLE
Arranged by DAN COATES

The Ballad of Gilligan's Isle - 3 - 1

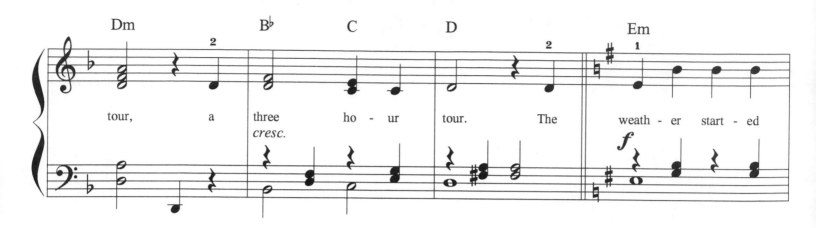

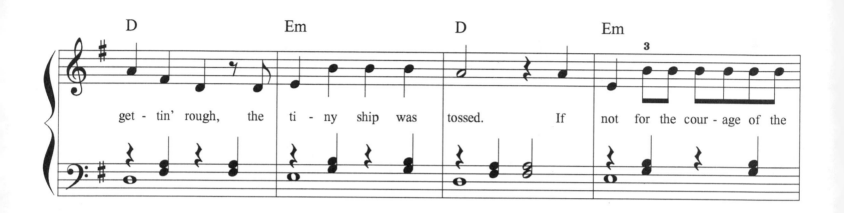

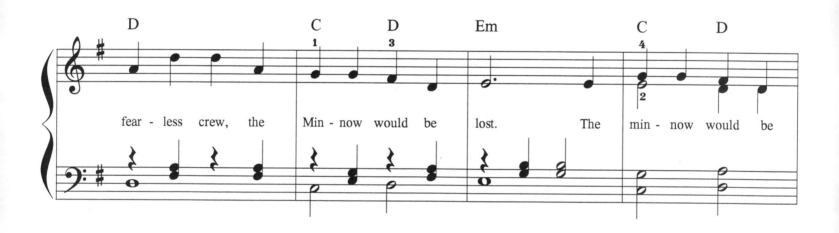

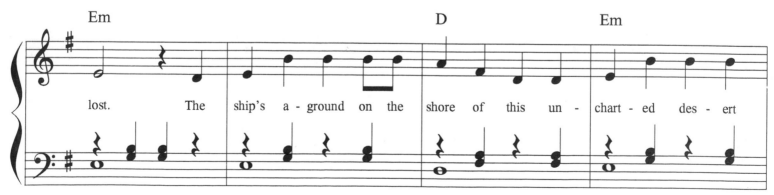

The Ballad of Gilligan's Isle - 3 - 2

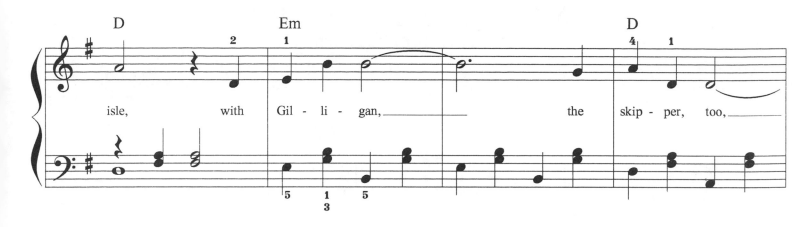

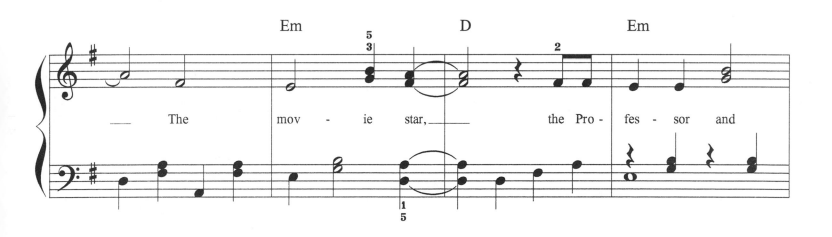

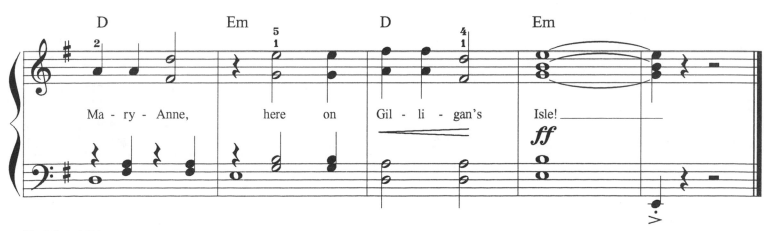

The Ballad of Gilligan's Isle - 3 - 3

From the Motion Picture "SUPERMAN"

CAN YOU READ MY MIND?
(Love Theme from "Superman")

Words by
LESLIE BRICUSSE

Music by
JOHN WILLIAMS
Arranged by DAN COATES

Moderate Ballad

Can you read my mind?

Do you know what it is you do to me?

Don't know who you are.

Just a friend from an-oth - er star. Here I

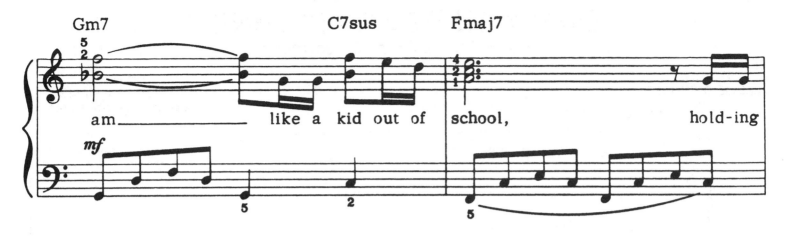

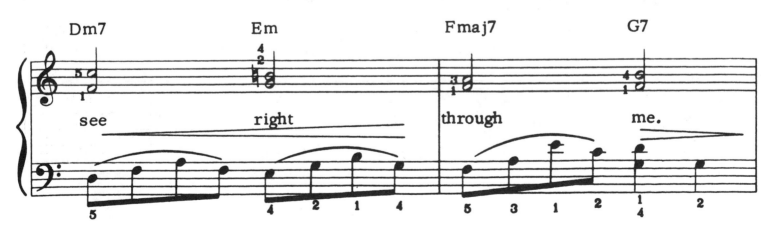

Featured in the M-G-M Picture "THE WIZARD OF OZ"

DING-DONG! THE WITCH IS DEAD

Lyrics by
E.Y. HARBURG

Music by
HAROLD ARLEN
Arranged by DAN COATES

Once there was a wicked witch in the lovely land of Oz, and a wicked-er, wicked-er, wicked-er witch there nev-er, nev-er was. She filled the folks in Munch-kin land with ter-ror and with dread, 'til

Ding-Dong! The Witch Is Dead - 4 - 1

MIGHTY MORPHIN POWER RANGERS

Words and Music by
SHUKI LEVY and KUSSA MAHCHI
Arranged by DAN COATES

Mighty Morphin Power Rangers - 2 - 1

Mighty Morphin Power Rangers - 2 - 2

I BELIEVE I CAN FLY

Words and Music by
R. KELLY
Arranged by DAN COATES

From the United Artists Picture "HOLE IN THE HEAD"

HIGH HOPES

Words by
SAMMY CAHN

Music by
JAMES VAN HEUSEN
Arranged by DAN COATES

1. Next time you're found_ with your chin on the ground,_ there's a
2. When trou-bles call _ and your back's to the wall, _ there's a

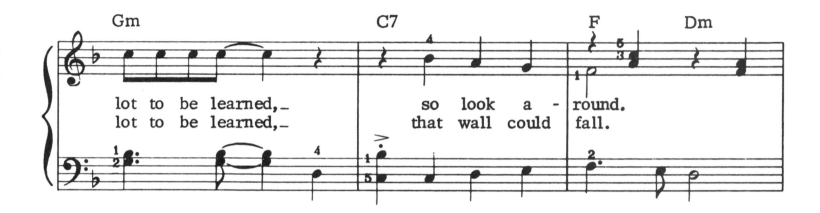

lot to be learned,_ so look a - round.
lot to be learned,_ that wall could fall.

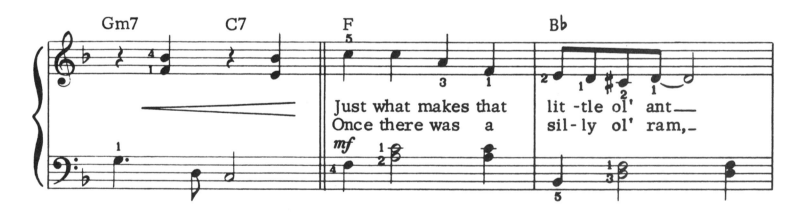

Just what makes that lit -tle ol' ant_
Once there was a sil-ly ol' ram,_

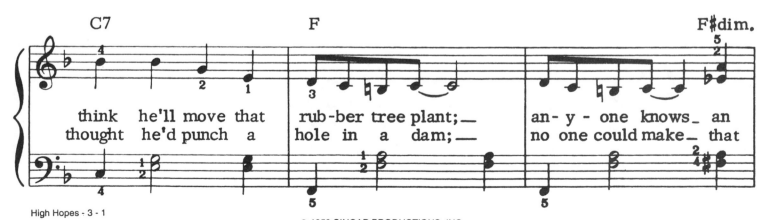

think he'll move that rub-ber tree plant;_ an-y-one knows_ an
thought he'd punch a hole in a dam;_ no one could make_ that

'stead of let - tin' go, just re- mem - ber that ant.
'stead of feel - in' sad, just re- mem - ber that ram.
they'll be burst - in' soon, they're just bound __ to go "pop!"

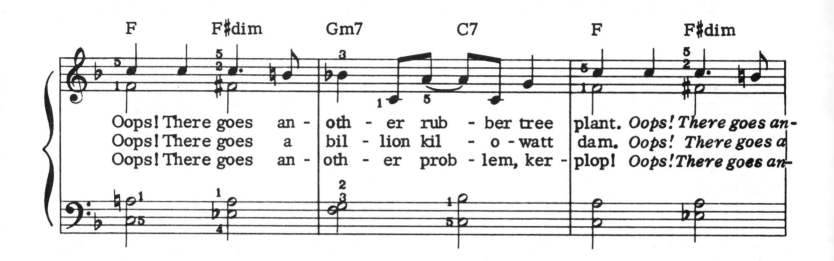

Oops! There goes an - oth - er rub - ber tree plant. *Oops! There goes an-*
Oops! There goes a bil - lion kil - o-watt dam. *Oops! There goes a*
Oops! There goes an - oth - er prob - lem, ker - plop! *Oops! There goes an-*

oth - er rub-ber tree plant. Oops! There goes an - oth - er rub - ber tree
bil-lion kil - o-watt dam. Oops! There goes a bil - lion kil - o - watt
oth - er prob-lem, ker-plop! Oops! There goes an - oth - er prob - lem, ker-

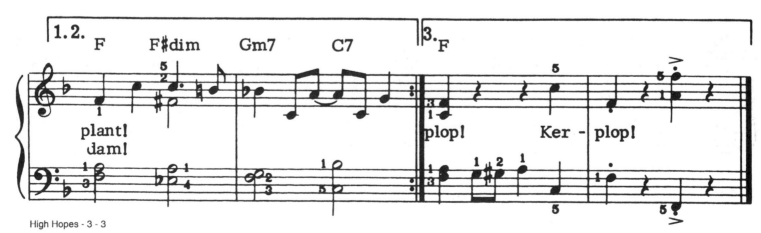

1.2.

plant!
dam!

3.

plop! Ker - plop!

Featured in the M-G-M Picture "THE WIZARD OF OZZ"

IF I ONLY HAD A BRAIN

Lyrics by
E.Y. HARBURG

Music by
HAROLD ARLEN
Arranged by DAN COATES

and per - haps I'd de-serve you and be ev - en wor - thy erv you if I

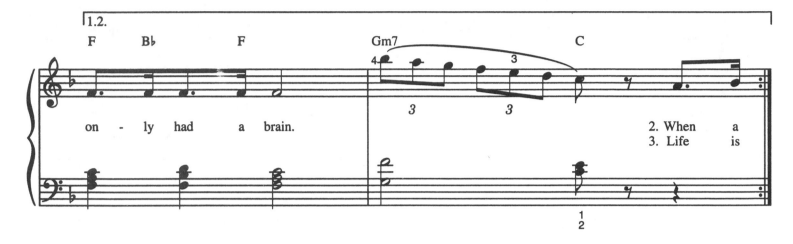

1.2.

on - ly had a brain.

2. When a
3. Life is

3.

on - ly had the nerve.

(Tin Woodman)

When a man's an empty kettle, he should be on his mettle and yet I'm torn apart
Just because I'm presumin' that I could be kinda human if I only had a heart.
I'd be tender, I'd be gentle and awful sentimental regarding love and art
I'd be friends with the sparrows and the boy that shoots the arrows, if I only had a heart.
Picture me a balcony, above a voice sings low, "Wherefore are thou, Romeo." I hear a beat. How sweet!
Just to register emotion. "Jealousy," "Devotion" and really feel the part
I would feel young and chipper and I'd lock it with a zipper if I only had a heart.

(Cowardly Lion)

Life is sad believe me missy when you're born to be a sissy, without the vim and verve
But I could change my habits, never more be scared of rabbits if I only had the nerve.
I'm afraid there's no denyin' I'm just a dandylion, a fate I don't deserve
But I could show my prowess, be a lion, not a mowess, if I only had the nerve.
Oh, I'd be in my stride, a king down to the core. Oh, I'd roar the way I'd never roared before,
and then I'd rrrwoof, and roar some more.
I would show the dinosaurus who's king around the forres', a king they better serve
Why with my regal beezer I could be another Caesar, if I only had the nerve.

If I Only Had a Brain - 3 - 3

Theme from "FRIENDS"

I'LL BE THERE FOR YOU

Words by
DAVID CRANE, MARTA KAUFFMAN, ALLEE WILLIS,
PHIL SOLEM and DANNY WILDE

Music by
MICHAEL SKLOFF
Arranged by DAN COATES

I'll Be There for You - 6 - 1

I'll Be There for You - 6 - 2

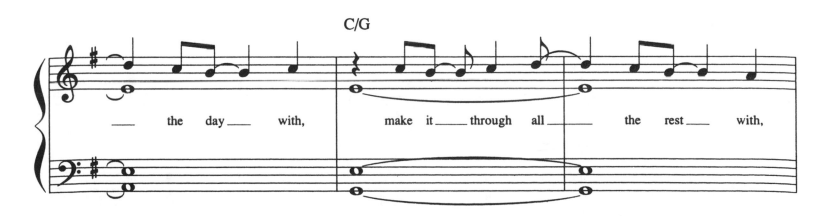

From the Twentieth Century Fox Motion Picture "ANASTASIA"

JOURNEY TO THE PAST

Lyrics by
LYNN AHRENS

Music by
STEPHEN FLAHERTY
Arranged by DAN COATES

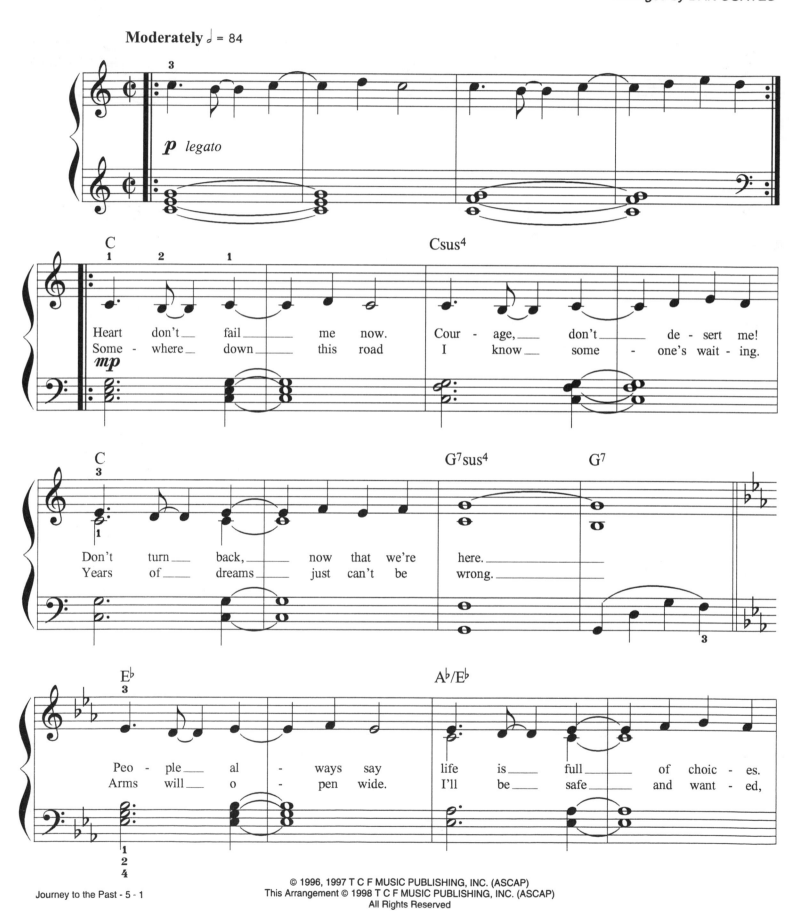

Moderately ♩ = 84

p legato

C
Csus4

Heart don't fail me now. Cour - age, don't de - sert me!
Some - where down this road I know some - one's wait - ing.

mp

C
G7sus4   G7

Don't turn back, now that we're here.
Years of dreams just can't be wrong.

Eb
Ab/Eb

Peo - ple al - ways say life is full of choic - es.
Arms will o - pen wide. I'll be safe and want - ed,

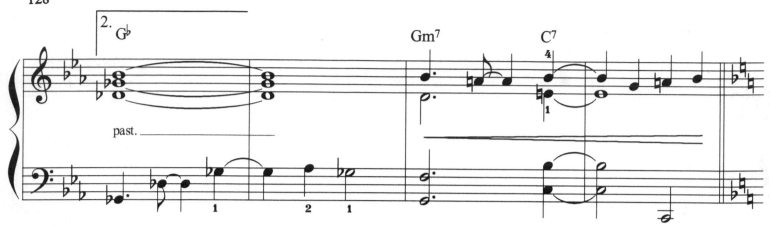

2. G♭   Gm⁷   C⁷

past.

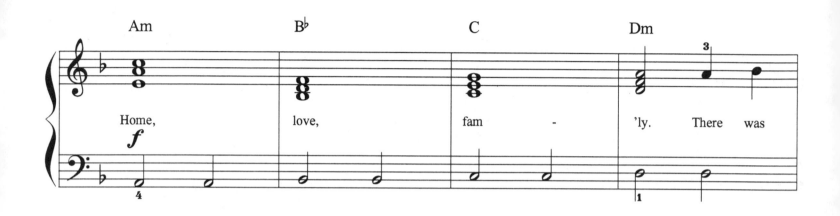

Am   B♭   C   Dm

Home,   love,   fam - 'ly.   There was

F/A   B♭   Csus⁴   C

once a time I   must have had them,   too.

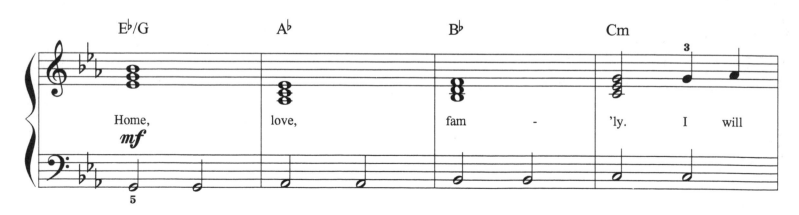

E♭/G   A♭   B♭   Cm

Home,   love,   fam - 'ly.   I will

never be com - plete un - til I find you. *cresc.*

ff

One step at a time. *mp*

One hope then an - oth - er. Who knows where this road may

go. Back to who I was. *mf*

On to find my fu - ture. Things my heart still needs to

From the Motion Picture "THE WIZARD OF OZ"

OVER THE RAINBOW

Words by
E.Y. HARBURG

Music by
HAROLD ARLEN
Arranged by DAN COATES

Over the Rainbow - 3 - 1

From the Lucasfilm Ltd. Production "RETURN OF THE JEDI" - A Twentieth Century-Fox Release.

LUKE AND LEIA

Music by
JOHN WILLIAMS
Arranged by DAN COATES

Luke and Leia - 2 - 1

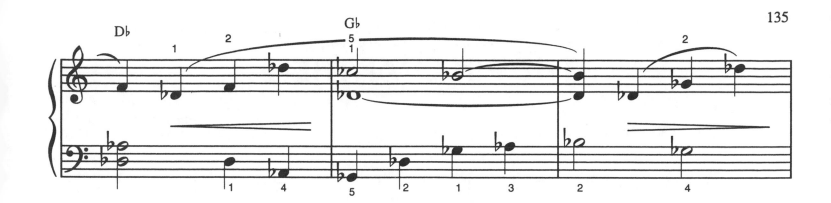

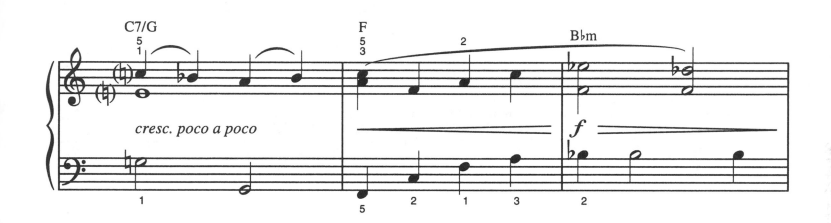

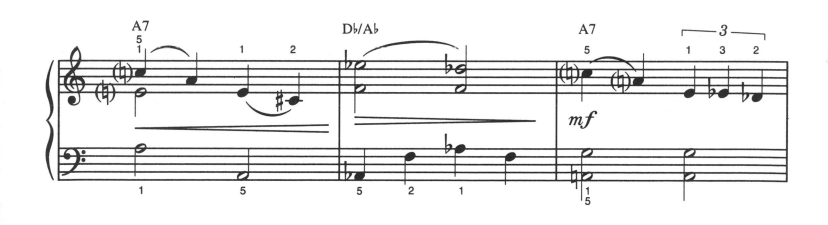

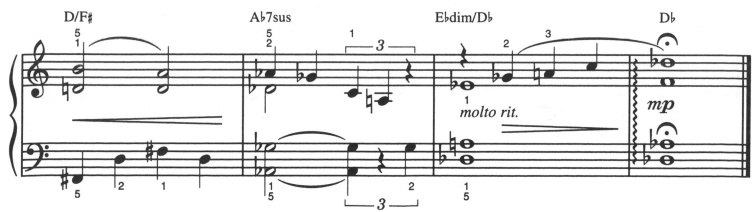

Luke and Leia - 2 - 2

Theme Song from the Mirisch-G&E Production, "THE PINK PANTHER," a United Artists Release

THE PINK PANTHER

Music by
HENRY MANCINI
Arranged by DAN COATES

The Pink Panther - 2 - 1

The Pink Panther - 2 - 2

*From the Lucasfilm Ltd. Productions "STAR WARS", "THE EMPIRE STRIKES BACK"
and "RETURN OF THE JEDI" - Twentieth Century-Fox Releases.*

STAR WARS
(Main Theme)

Music by
JOHN WILLIAMS
Arranged by DAN COATES

Star Wars - 2 - 1

From the Warner Bros. Motion Picture "SUPERMAN"

THEME FROM "SUPERMAN"

Music by
JOHN WILLIAMS
Arranged by DAN COATES

Theme From "Superman" - 3 - 1

Theme From "Superman" - 3 - 2

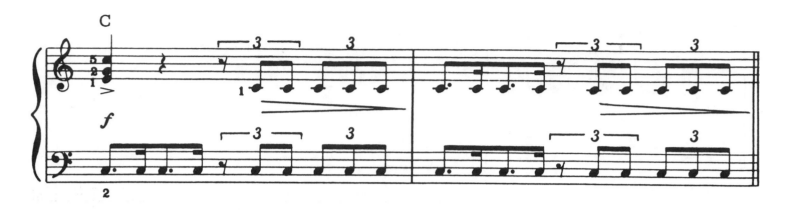

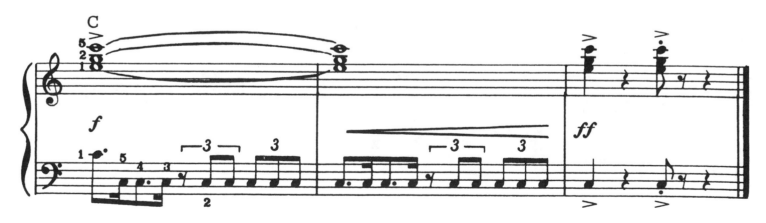

Theme From "Superman" - 3 - 3

Featured in the M-G-M Picture "THE WIZARD OF OZ"

WE'RE OFF TO SEE THE WIZARD
(The Wonderful Wizard of Oz)

Lyric by
E.Y. HARBURG

Music by
HAROLD ARLEN
Arranged by DAN COATES

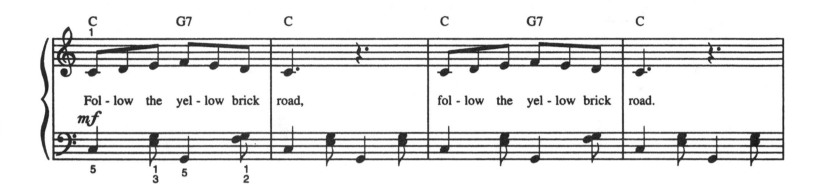

Fol - low the yel - low brick road, fol - low the yel - low brick road.

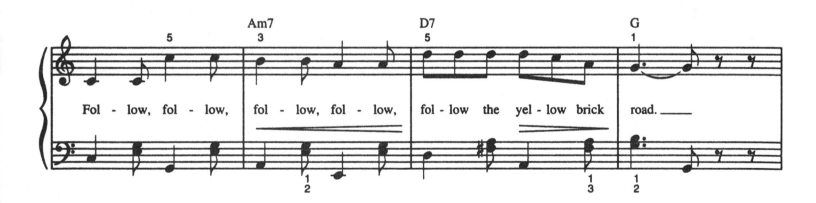

Fol - low, fol - low, fol - low, fol - low, fol - low the yel - low brick road.

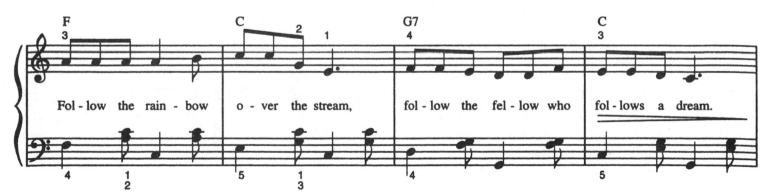

Fol - low the rain - bow o - ver the stream, fol - low the fel - low who fol - lows a dream.

We're Off to See the Wizard - 3 - 1

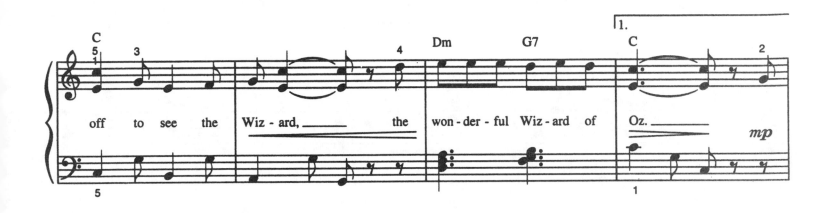

We're off to See the Wizard - 3 - 3

From the Twentieth Century Fox Motion Picture
"ANASTASIA"

AT THE BEGINNING

Lyrics by
LYNN AHRENS

Music by
STEPHEN FLAHERTY
Arranged by DAN COATES

At the Beginning - 5 - 1

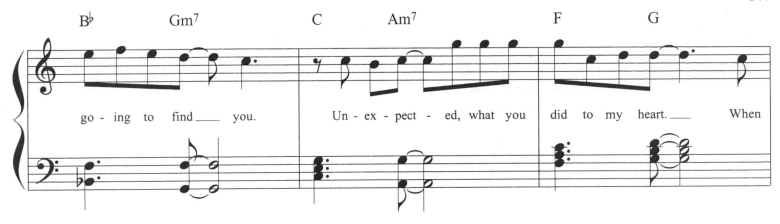

going to find___ you. Un - ex - pect - ed, what you did to my heart.___ When

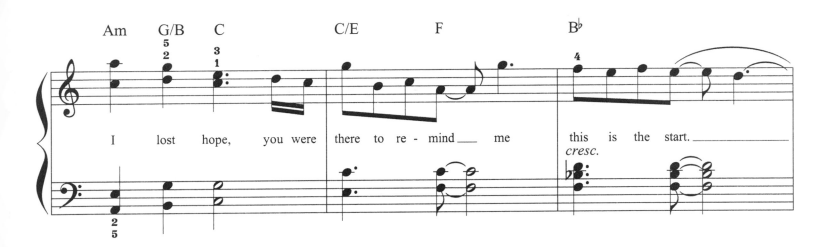

I lost hope, you were there to re - mind___ me this is the start.___
cresc.

And life is a road, and I want to keep go - ing. Love is a riv - er, I want to keep flow - ing.
mf

Life is a road, now and for - ev - er. Won - der - ful jour - ney! I'll be there when the world stops turn - ing,

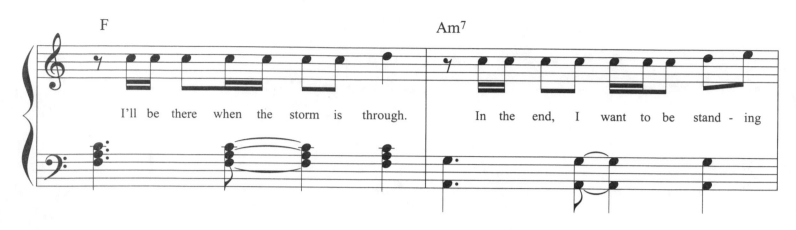

I'll be there when the storm is through.
In the end, I want to be stand - ing

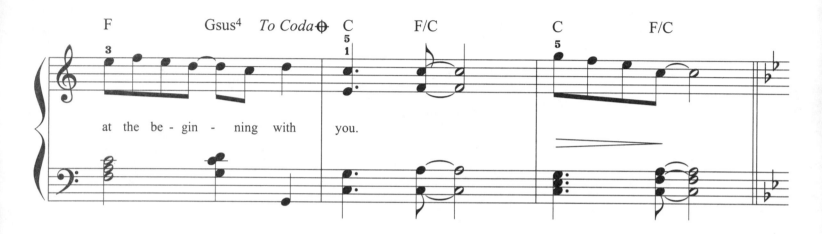

at the be - gin - ning with you.

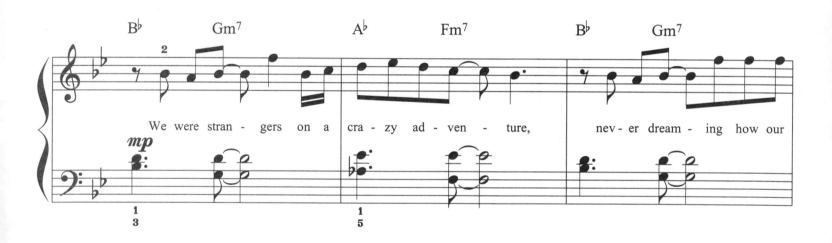

We were stran - gers on a cra - zy ad - ven - ture,
nev - er dream - ing how our

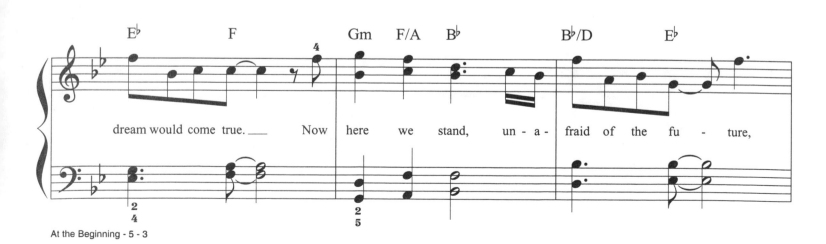

dream would come true. ___ Now here we stand, un - a - fraid of the fu - ture,

Dan Coates

One of today's foremost personalities in the field of printed music, Dan Coates has been providing teachers and professional musicians with quality piano material since 1975. Equally adept in arranging for beginners or accomplished musicians, his Big Note, Easy Piano and Professional Touch arrangements have made a significant contribution to the industry.

Born in Syracuse, New York, Dan began to play piano at age four. By the time he was 15, he'd won a New York State competition for music composers. After high school graduation, he toured the United States, Canada and Europe as an arranger and pianist with the world-famous group "Up With People".

Dan settled in Miami, Florida, where he studied piano with Ivan Davis at the University of Miami while playing professionally throughout southern Florida. To date, his performance credits include appearances on "Murphy Brown," "My Sister Sam" and at the Opening Ceremonies of the 1984 Summer Olympics in Los Angeles. Dan has also accompanied such artists as Dusty Springfield and Charlotte Rae.

In 1982, Dan began his association with Warner Bros. Publications - an association which has produced more than 400 Dan Coates books and sheets. Throughout the year he conducts piano workshops nation-wide, during which he demonstrates his popular arrangements.